POETRY MONSTERS

Amazing Rhymes

Edited By Debbie Killingworth

First published in Great Britain in 2020 by:

Young Writers
Remus House
Coltsfoot Drive
Peterborough
PE2 9BF
Telephone: 01733 890066
Website: www.youngwriters.co.uk

Book Design by Ashley Janson

Softback ISBN 978-1-83928-694-0

Printed and bound in the UK by BookPrintingUK
Website: www.bookprintinguk.com
YB0429M

FOREWORD

Hello Reader!

For our latest poetry competition we sent out funky and vibrant worksheets for primary school pupils to fill in and create their very own poem about fiendish fiends and crazy creatures. I got to read them and guess what? They were **roarsome**!

The pupils were able to read our example poems and use the fun-filled free resources to help bring their imaginations to life, and the result is pages **oozing** with exciting poetic tales. From friendly monsters to mean monsters, from bumps in the night to **rip-roaring** adventures, these pupils have excelled themselves, and now have the joy of seeing their work in print!

Here at Young Writers we love nothing more than poetry and creativity. We aim to encourage children to put pen to paper to inspire a love of the written word and explore their own unique worlds of creativity. We'd like to congratulate all of the aspiring authors that have created this book of **monstrous mayhem** and we know that these poems will be enjoyed for years to come. So, dive on in and submerge yourself in all things furry and fearsome (and perhaps check under the bed!).

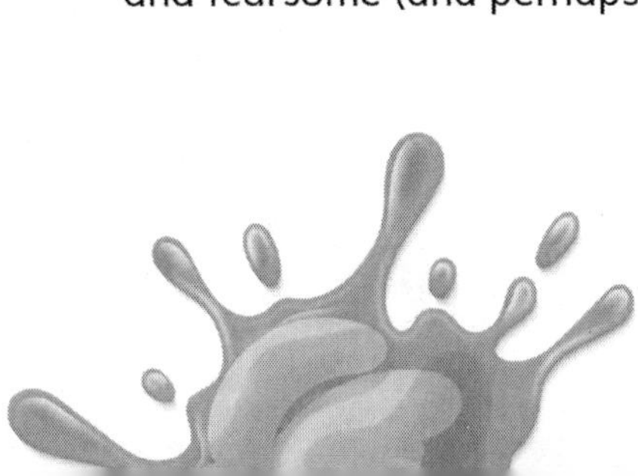

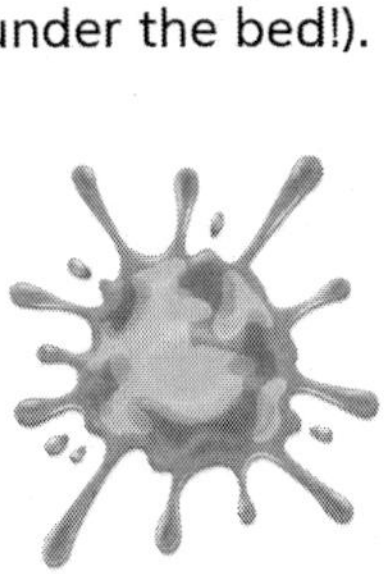

CONTENTS

Conor O Brolcháin (8) 61
Aliona Ní Mhaoláin (7) 62
Chloe Ní Mhuirí (9) 63
Braiden Ní Labhraí (9) 64
Riley Mag Aoidh (8) 65
Aoife Nic Congail (9) 66
Ellie-Mai de Craig (8) 67
Avril Ní Chárthaigh (7) 68
Yasmin Ní Mhaolaín (7) 69
Dara Mac Aoidh (9) 70
Brooke Ní Ghliasáin-Ní Ghabhann (7) 71

Old Sarum Primary School, Old Sarum

Isabella Mitchell (8) 72
Elliot Smith (9) 73
Elly-Mae Willock (10) 74
Dylan Thomas Chandler (7) 75
Aya Bendhiyaf (10) 76
Skye Thomas (9) 77
Jasmine Pemberton (6) 78
Chloe Kimberly Baker (7) 79
Beau (6) 80
Isabella Beauchamp (7) 81
Jessica Davies (6) 82
Eloise Kennedy (10) 83

St Bartholomew's CE Primary School, Stourport-On-Severn

Patsy Griffiths (8), Alfie & Lucus Connolly (8) 84
Ben Ellis (9) 85
Finley Ashdown (8) 86
Melody Bryant (8) 87
Yazmin Newton (8) 88
Macie Crumpton (8) 89
Adriana Gabalaite (8) 90
Katelyn Mason (9) 91
Olly Kendrick (8) 92
Isabelle (8) 93
Ollie Howard Curzey (8) 94
Olivia Mitchell (9) 95
Laytton Loveridge (8) 96
Lacey May Webb (8) 97
Liberty Middleton (8) 98
Phoebe Southwick (8) 99
Sophie Holly Webb (8) 100
Mia Grace Jones (8) 101
Faustas Augys (8) 102
Elliot Taylor (8) 103
Autumn Joy Birch (8) 104
Jazmin Bower (8) 105

St Martin's CE (VA) Primary School, Fangfoss

Abigail Bartle (7) 106
Esme Thomas (7) 108
Archie Sissons (8) 109
Emma Rebecca Curtis (8) 110
Oliver Eden Harrison (7) 111
William Alexander Brack (7) 112
Kuba Cierniak (7) 113
Lotty Harrison (7) 114
Evelyn May Anne Baxter (7) 115
Daniel Bell (7) 116
Henry Thomas Duncan (7) 117
Elsa Grace Rogers (7) 118
Tom Lee (7) 119
Courtney G (8) 120

Wilshere Dacre Junior Academy, Hitchin

Susan Turley (7) 121
Olivia Matthews (7) 122
Emma Whiting (8) 124
Joshua Morgan (7) 125
Laya Mae Green (7) 126
Lucas Young (7) 127
India-Mae Noone (7) 128
Elizabeth Dennis (7) 129
Eva Winstanley (7) 130
Myla Rose Gorski-Eaton (7) 131
Sophie Jeffrey (8) 132

Gabrielle Bernice Odiana (7) 133
Harveer Singh Nijjar (7) 134
Ben Evans (7) 135
James Hull (8) 136
Keira Robinson (7) 137
Jackson Donnelly (8) 138
Leonardo Dainton-Cadona (7) 140
Emma Fenwick (7) 141
Max Folbigg (7) 142
Anne Coles Barrett (7) 143
Imogen Stubbs (8) 144
Stanley Buckland (7) 145
Jack Cummins (7) 146
Flynn Jenkinson (7) 147
Fawzia Quddus (8) 148
Edward Salmond (7) 149
Sophia Scheepers (7) 150
Jonah Blue (7) 151
Ellie-May Needham (8) 152
Joshua Jeeves (7) 153
Eva Carelli 154
Ronnie Harris-Dawes (7) 155
Erin Hart (8) 156
Isabella Evans (7) 157
Luca William Jones (8) 158

Ysgol Brynaerau, Pontllyfni

Dion Connah (10) 159
Alisha Leigh Becker (11) 160
Hari Carroll (8) 163
Tomi Williams (10) 165
Elisha Hayes (11) 167
Celt Pritchard-Jones (9) 169
Jarno Burgess (10) 171
Osian Hywel Roberts (9) 173
Bethany Whitear (8) 175
Nanw MacIntyre Huws (8) 177
Lleucu Haf Williams (10) 179
Sara Carroll (8) 181
Rhydian Hildige (9) 183
Betsan Cim Evans (10) 185
Lily Erin Millen (8) 187
Morgan Llyr Davies (9) 189
Elan Llyfni Fon Jones (8) 191
Carys-Wyn Pass (9) 193
Kimberly Jones (9) 195
Arawn Dylan Morus (10) 197
Meilir Rhun Davies (9) 199

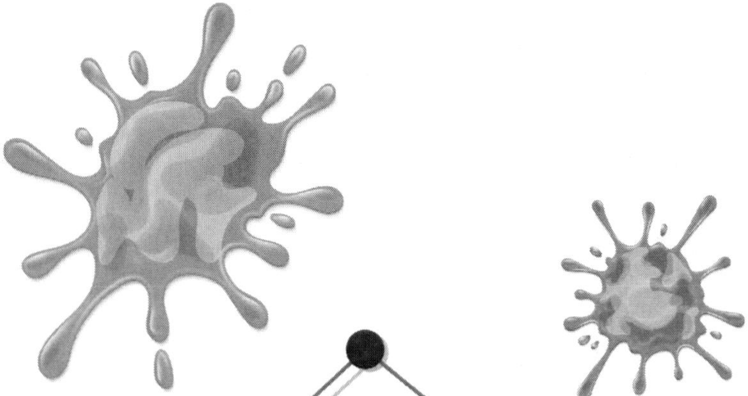

THE POEMS

Cheeky Little Monster

I have my dinner,
Go to the bathroom
And come back...
"Where's my dinner, Amber?"
I find her with sticky, icky hands -
Eating my dinner

I sit on the sofa,
Who is behind me?
Amber's behind me... "Boo!"

It's time for bed,
We all sleep.
At 7am she's down the stairs playing with her blocks.

"Oh no! I have to go."
I leave the house.
She starts to cry,
"Oh Amber, I love you!"

Pippa May Oglesby (8)
Caslon Primary Community School, Halesowen

Sash The Scary Monster

There once was a monster,
He said his name was Sash,
He once was a person
But he got in a crash.

He is hairy,
He's a little smelly,
He is quite scary
And he has a big belly.

But one day
I couldn't find him,
I heard him say,
"I'm over here."

I found him in the washing machine,
He was very clean,
I saw he'd split,
I couldn't seal the seam.
Oh Sash, oh Sash, oh Sash!

Alicia Jane Spence (8)
Caslon Primary Community School, Halesowen

My Monster

There was a monster called Nightmare
He likes to frighten people
He scratches people so hard that they bleed
He bites people so hard they have to go to hospital
He steals people's money
He puts people in jail for hours
And he chases criminals
He swaps Coca-Cola with vinegar
And someone drinks it and they die
My monster crashes into things
He is a funny monster
He is my best friend.

Hannah Louise Victoria Sprintall (8)
Caslon Primary Community School, Halesowen

Ewie The Gooey Monster

Ewie is a gooey monster.
He likes to scare girls and boys.
He makes a lot of noise.

I tell him not to scare people anymore
But he just keeps on making lots of loud roars.

I told him to be nice
But he just said, "No!"
And continued to pinch my pet mice.

Ewie is a gooey monster
That makes a lot of noise.
I love you Ewie the gooey monster!

Bella Young (8)
Caslon Primary Community School, Halesowen

The Unusual Monster

It doesn't walk, it runs.
It doesn't jump, it leaps.
It's never that fun,
So don't make a peep.
Or here it comes to sleep.
It likes to eat,
It might think you're meat.
Oh no, here it comes
It looks like defeat.
But no it's just my little sister,
She has come to say goodnight.

Under my bed,
There it lies.

Alexander Hulston (9)
Caslon Primary Community School, Halesowen

Bad Ziggy

Ziggy is a Halloween monster,
A scary, hairy Halloween monster.
I'm sitting on my bed,
Ziggy is eating my lollipops!
Stop, stop!
I'm lying down,
I feel a spiky claw ripping my teds!
Stop, stop!
He boos my brother,
Stop, stop!
We pay money,
Ziggy destroys things
But I'll always love my monster.

Layla Rafiq (8)
Caslon Primary Community School, Halesowen

I'm Related To A Monster

She isn't evil,
She isn't a devil.

She likes to play
With me all day.

She is my best friend
And our friendship will never end.

She is always taking selfies of her dog
And her dog is always chasing frogs.

And so indeed, she's not a monster,
She is my sixteen-year-old big sister!

Mellieha Letts (8)
Caslon Primary Community School, Halesowen

My Monster

She is cuddly.
She is nice.
She is cute.
She is bright.
She is clean.
She is on time.
She is fluffy.
She is fine.
She is squishy.
She is kind.
She is Mrs Cutey
And she is mine.
She is sweet.
She is mine.
She is neat.
She's all mine.
I really love my monster.

Laurie Sprigg (8)
Caslon Primary Community School, Halesowen

Mushy The Monster

My monster may sound bad,
She may look a little mad
But she's so cute.
She has a little toot!
She likes to play sport
But she's very short.
She has wobbly legs
And plays with pegs.
She also has double arms
And red palms.

Nadr Zaid (8)
Caslon Primary Community School, Halesowen

Monster School

My monster's name is Muffin,
She is cute, fluffy and friendly,
She has got blue eyes,
She is sometimes lazy
And she sometimes scares people.
I say to her, "Stop scaring people,"
But I do love her!

Areeba Batool Ahmad (8)
Caslon Primary Community School, Halesowen

The Rap Monster!

My name is Nameless
And I am flameless.
I am famous
And I am painless.
I have gold chains around my neck.

Yeah boy, got my Lambo,
Got my monster!

I'm a rap monster!

Dominic Lane (8)
Caslon Primary Community School, Halesowen

Happy Halloween

The leaves are falling from the trees
And the wind gives off such a cool breeze.
Happy Halloween you guys, he he he!
The sun is beaming with light,
The children are screaming with fright!
I wonder if it is going to be a full moon tonight.
Happy Halloween you guys, he he he!
The spiders are hunting for a new home
And some have spun a web around the garden
gnome.
Happy Halloween you guys, he he he!
The children are pulling out pumpkin brains
To celebrate Halloween and play all the fun
games!
Trick or treat is the worst of all
When we have to knock on doors
And sing 'trick or treat, smell my feet
Give me something nice to eat'.
Happy Halloween you guys, he he he!
Then comes the night, the spookiest of all
When the ghosts and ghouls come out to be fools

The dogs turn into werewolves, the cats turn into bats
The fish turn into toads and the rabbits turn into rats!
Happy Halloween you guys, he he he!
And all of this, for just one night!
What is it for?
I am already in fright!
Well the truth is my friend
Halloween is just a joke
It is all about scaring away ghosts
Happy Halloween you guys, he he he!
Enjoy your sweets and treats!

Lilly-Peach Dorethy Rhodes (8)
Castle Primary School, Mow Cop

Slime All Around

Peeping through the darkness,
Waiting to catch some kids,
He has slimy jaws
Just like his amazing slimy paws.
In the daylight Slimy appears
Everywhere in sight,
And in the day he is okay and fine
At night he has a mighty might
With a super strong bite.
Sometimes he is too angry
And chops the houses down
But when he is sad he has a mighty frown.
In the city he doesn't follow the laws
So he just relies on his paws.
When Josh is happy he goes to play
But he doesn't play in the park
He plays at the bay.

Alexander James Watson (7)
Castle Primary School, Mow Cop

My Secret Monster

My monster's name is Jaws
And he has really big claws.
He lives under my bed
With my teddy named Fred.
He comes out at night
When out goes the light
But not to bite
But to say goodnight.

Danielle Cooper (9)
Castle Primary School, Mow Cop

Pig The Naughty Digger

My monster is monstrous.
He is called Pig.
His favourite thing to do is to dig, dig, dig.
He has a friend called Tig
Who also likes to dig.
He is probably digging now...
Are you?

Sophie Atkinson (8)
Castle Primary School, Mow Cop

Sleyer

S uper creepy.
L umps around your yard.
E ats your dreams.
Y ounglings should beware!
E volves over time and
R uns on water!

Douglas Harrison Mitchell (8)
Castle Primary School, Mow Cop

Look Out, Luke Is About

He stares furiously at you while you're in bed with his humongous fifteen eyes when you least expect it.
Look at his four sharp-as-knife teeth crunching down on your favourite toys while you're fast asleep.
His bright orange and green fur blows in the dead of night while he walks through the street when everyone else is sleeping.
Watch his huge feet bang off the ground every step you feel the ground, watch out!
Stay away from him or he will step on you.
As he walks through each bright street light you see his terrifying sharp horns.
They are as sharp as knives, watch out!
His hands row back and forward as he takes each huge step you see his sharp claws while his hands row.
As I said, look out, Luke is about!

Nicole Cairns (8)
Forehill Primary School, Ayr

Fluffy Freya

F reya is the most friendly monster ever.
L ook at her bright blue eyes as blue as water.
U nder her fluffy fur she is like a rainbow.
F reya lives in the magical rainforest.
F irst she liked eating kids now she eats teachers.
Y ellow makes Freya go mad.

F reya has loads of rabbit friends like her.
R ed and bright pink are her favourite colours.
E very bunny in the world is her friend.
Y abo is her favourite drink.
A nnabelle is her best friend.

Katie Brown (8)
Forehill Primary School, Ayr

The Creeper

Creepy Creeper,
Watch out he will eat you, even a child.
Rotten Creeper is super smelly, just like junk.
He's coming for you and he'll eat like it's a KFC.
With his ugly one eyeball it's the Creeper.
With his grumpy face he'll scare you.
He's as green as Shrek and as strong as everyone.
He'll rip out your guts.
He lives in a forest.
Mostly he kills whatever he sees.
He's never helpful, not even to himself.
He has 2,000 jaws
He'll eat his family.
He drinks slime.

Freddie Murray (8)
Forehill Primary School, Ayr

The Terrible Trooper

Hear him squelch on the swamp where he lives.
See him coming towards you.
You will faint in an instant.
Smell his slimy, greasy body,
It's the most disgusting smell in the world.
Silently he sneaks up behind you.
He doesn't eat you, he scares you.

He lives in a horror land as scary as a killer clown.
He is a joker, a big one.

He has a friend and a foe.
His friend is called Munch Monster
And his foe is called Clever Crook.

Watch out children, don't have nightmares!

Samuel Hunt (8)
Forehill Primary School, Ayr

Mischievous Monster Mannie

Watch her eyes scream in horror.
Red and as bright and red as blood.
Her skin is as black as coal.
She looks so cuddly,
But it's a trick don't you know?
Her mouth blowing out poisonous gas
Watch out! Don't breathe it in.
Her face, oh not her face, her faces!
Yes three, so scary and mean!
Her arms glowing, dripping nails down.
Don't stand underneath her,
Make sure you don't get hit by a giant nail!
She can shapeshift into a human.
She can be anything she wants to be.

Milly Mason (7)
Forehill Primary School, Ayr

Mikey The Monster

There is a monster,
A chubby monster.
He has yellow, yucky teeth.
Crazily he chomps terrible tree trunks.
His belly button is full of dog food,
As sticky as ear wax.
He has pointy claws,
They are like vampire fangs.
His eyes are as large as Mount Everest.
An antenna is on his armpit.
His armpits are as smelly as a wombat's bottom.
He has twelve legs.
His spikes are as long as a bee's stinger.
There is a monster,
A chubby monster
And he's under your desk!

Zach Gordon (7)
Forehill Primary School, Ayr

The Scary, Hairy Monster

There is a monster,
A scary monster.
He has black scary teeth.
He has ear wax in his belly button.
Disgustingly he chomps smelly fish.
His eyes blink as quick as a bear.
He is as fat as a blue whale.
His claws are as sharp as a dinosaur's claws.
His hair is as sharp as sharp stone.
His tail is as scaly as a snake.
His nose is as flat as a pancake.
His head is as flat as a bin lid.

There is a monster,
A scary monster
And he is looking for you.

Sophie Clark (8)
Forehill Primary School, Ayr

A Story Of A Tall, Spooky Monster

There is a monster,
A fierce monster.
He has brown disgusting fangs,
He chomps big logs the size of boulders,
His belly button is as sticky as ear wax,
His head is like a vampire head,
He has big eyes, he will stare at you,
His nose is as small as a mouse,
The monster's arms are as creepy as a spider,
Disgustingly his feet are as smelly as rotten rats.
The monster's name is Jamie.
This is a monster,
A scary monster
And he is in my house.

Dylan O'Brien (8)
Forehill Primary School, Ayr

Meet Monster Joe

M eet Monster Joe,
O r if you're not nice he will eat you.
N ow it is dinner time, he eats green and yellow slime.
S ometimes he stares at you with his loopy eyes.
T ommy is his big brother, he looks horrendous.
E mily is his nice sister.
R em is his disgusting stepdad.

J oe is seven years old.
O nly if he loses a game he would get in a rage.
"E cho?" his dad shouted. It was scary!

Daniel O'Lone (7)
Forehill Primary School, Ayr

Shante The Horror

Silently he crunches on the boring bones of teachers.
Listen to the terrifying screams coming from the blood-covered basement of the school.
Dare you to go in the portal to Tremendous Town?
He lives there.
Shante is the king of horror.
Slickly he jumps out from under the creaky bed determinedly.
Look at the knife with blood on.
His smell is so bad that you can faint pale white.
He creeps through the night into the school.
He does not die.

Blair Paterson (8)
Forehill Primary School, Ayr

Muddy Buddy

A muddy body with a mouse head.
Four bloody mouths,
One on his mucky belly.
Three on his face.
Red eyes in a swamp.
Big ears, legs like logs on a birch tree.
Two tails, sharp claws on his hands.

I saw him in the deep swamp.
I said, "I can smell the muck.
I can hear the big stomps in the mud."

Muddy the monster eats people that come near him.
I have proof that he is real.
Watch out!

Daniel Morarkas (8)
Forehill Primary School, Ayr

The Mischievous Monster

There is a monster,
A cheeky monster.
He has hairy, scary, purple fur.
His head is as round as a burst ball.
Horribly he gobbles grass.
His nose is as long as a dragon's tooth.
His tummy is so plump,
Disgustingly full with food.
Quickly his tiny legs run.
His feet are as bright as the sun.
His toes are as tiny as a mouse.
There is a monster,
A cheeky monster
And he's coming to find you!

Lily Carly Freeburn (8)
Forehill Primary School, Ayr

The Ugly Monster

There is a monster,
A spiky monster.
He showed me his legs, ewww!
He's hairy, his hair is 10cm.
He chomps spiders.
His horns are brown.
His eyes are red.
His spikes are dark blue.
His hands are as sticky as glue.
His teeth are long - they're 12cm.
He's so ugly he has spots all over him
That are pink and black.
There is a monster,
A spiky monster
And he's behind you!

Tess Diane Black (8)
Forehill Primary School, Ayr

Lillabelle The Monster

There is a monster,
A pretty monster.
She has glittery, green skin.
Happily she glows it in the dark.
She is as thin as a fish.
She has big amazing antennae,
They are green as well.
Quickly she sips shiny hot chocolate,
It stays in her hand quietly.
Her arms are as bony as a skeleton.
Kindly she hugs you nicely.
There is a monster,
A pretty monster
And she's beside you!

Emily Grace Graham (8)
Forehill Primary School, Ayr

Smelly Sam

There is a monster,
A smelly monster.
He has brown, rotten teeth.
Sam's smelly belly button with revolting hair inside.
His head is as flat as a bin lid,
That's what makes him smell.
Small, scaly eyes Sam has.
He has horrid horns as long as a lion's claw.
Sam's nose is long like a rat's tail.
There is a monster,
A smelly monster
And he's my friend!

Lori Thorburn (8)
Forehill Primary School, Ayr

Frank The Fierce Monster

There is a monster,
A fierce monster.
He has ugly, sharp ears.
Disgustingly he has white and jaggy horns.
He has orange night eyes.
He has long arms like an anaconda.
His feet are as short as a rough rat's skin.
Strangely his belly button is full of hair,
It's stuck on with saliva.
There is a monster,
A fierce monster
And he's looking for you.

Luke Reid (7)
Forehill Primary School, Ayr

The Fierce Monster

There is a monster,
A very large monster.
He has teeth as sharp as knives.
While gobbling down a rotten rat
Loudly his feet stomp like the ground is rumbling.
His three eyes look away suspiciously.
Disgustingly slimy snotters come running out of his nose.
When he smells his prey off he goes.
There is a monster,
A very large monster
And he's under my bed.

Holly Gallagher (8)
Forehill Primary School, Ayr

Fred The Scaly Monster

There is a monster,
A scaly monster.
His teeth are as pointy as a sword.
Disturbingly he devours disgusting slugs and snails.
His scales are rock solid.
His head is as oval as an egg.
His fingers as fat as chips.
He's as smelly as a slimy serpent.
His nose is flat like a pancake.
There is a monster,
A scaly monster
And he's coming for you!

Charlotte Meek (8)
Forehill Primary School, Ayr

The Catcobra!

Look, the Catcobra,
deep in the sea with her grey, dark gloomy eyes.
Behold the black scars all over her face.

See her sharp orange teeth
viciously tearing apart the dolphin's skin
while her eyes watch for more prey.
The Catcobra is the size of buildings
and can easily destroy cities with her webs
while her giant spider legs rampage through
buildings.

Adam Maxwell (8)
Forehill Primary School, Ayr

Slimy The Monster

There is a monster,
A slimy monster.
Creepily his scary eyes stare at you.
His size is as big as a lamp post.
He is as wide as a shed.
He has yellow, sharp teeth,
Disgustingly, he devours his fish.
Oddly his belly button is full of boogers.
His horns are as pointy as a thorn.
There is a monster,
A slimy monster
And he's coming for you!

Mia Bersales (8)
Forehill Primary School, Ayr

The Flesh-Chomping Monster

There is a monster,
A scaly monster.
He has horrible yellow toenails
That are filled with dirt.
His feet are as smelly as the sewers.
He's as fat as an elephant.
Grossly he chomps on chihuahuas.
His belly button is stuffed with slime.
It's as sticky as super glue.
There is a monster,
A scaly monster
And he's coming for you!

Ben MacPherson (8)
Forehill Primary School, Ayr

Ugly

There is a monster,
An ugly monster
And she is so bright.
You can't look
But she's not nice.
She scares you in your sleep,
She does not like happy.
The monster eats raw fish
And smells like it too.
The kid who lives there,
The kid gets scared at night.
There is a monster,
An ugly monster
And she's in your house.

Sophie Madden (8)
Forehill Primary School, Ayr

The Mouldy Monster

See the monster walking down the road at night,
peeking in your window.
Watch the Mouldy Monster steal precious things
that belong to you.
I can see brown and black patches shining in your
window.
I am watching the mould fall off the monster's
manky dress.
Feel the air fly through the window as slow as a
tortoise.
Be silent, if not you are going to be rude.

Hannah Walters (8)
Forehill Primary School, Ayr

Moshey The Monster

Moshey the monster creeps around the house.
On the chair she sits holding her blood soup.
Her four eyes are as dark as coal.
She has twelve teeth,
So watch out she likes the blood of humans!
Her four ears can hear you in every room
So she can creep up on you
And grab you in her jaws.

So watch out,
Moshey can see you in her mind!

Ava Rodger (8)
Forehill Primary School, Ayr

Sienna The Blood-Sucking Monster

Look at her sharp blood-covered teeth, eating mums.
The one foot has six toes and twelve spots that will explode.
Its triangular nose has a wart that is full of pus.
Look, its slimy body is melting.
Its horns are like arms with hands.
Her eyes are cute but she is vicious.
She's shaped like a ghost but she's a monster.

Melissa Love (8)
Forehill Primary School, Ayr

Jennifer The Gooey Monster

There is a monster,
A gooey monster.
She has two big, ugly, warted feet.
Her horns are as slimy as saliva!
Up her hairy, horrible nose
It's stuffed with snotters!
As loud as a lion,
She storms outside with her loud large feet.
There is a monster,
A gooey monster
And she is coming for you!

Gemma Campbell (8)
Forehill Primary School, Ayr

The Chuky Cheese Monster

Don't look into his bright red eyes.
If you dare to look into the Chuky Cheese Monster's eyes
They are shaped as a crosshair and will shoot fireballs at you in a flash.
His red blood-covered teeth will crunch your bones in a millisecond.
His ears are as good at hearing as you are at screaming at the sight of him!

Max Doolan (8)
Forehill Primary School, Ayr

Blob The Children Monster

His tentacles are so long at night.
He will grab you at night and crunch your bones to shreds.
Look at the sharp horns on his head, as sharp as a knife.
The spiky, horrendous, dirty claws in your back garden.
Look at his stripy tail, dripping blood all over.
Dripping blood all over, covering his body.

Anna Muir (8)
Forehill Primary School, Ayr

Temper The Bone Cruncher

Watch him stare at you with his dripping eyes.
Full of bloody teeth coming right at your dark, gloomy face.
Looking about for teachers ready to crunch on their bones.
He quietly looks around classrooms from right to left.
Look out, the monster cruncher is about.

Dylan Neil (8)
Forehill Primary School, Ayr

Mischievous Monster

One gloomy night the Minotaur was lurking house to house,
Taking children, food, pets and whoever he wants.
When he gets back to his den he eats what he took.
He looks like a bull with muscular legs and has teeth as sharp as a knife.

Shae Mackie (8)
Forehill Primary School, Ayr

Fantastic Fangs

Look at her sharp fangs getting ready to hunt.
Her poisonous spikes are ready to kill.
Amazing metallic scales shimmering in the sunshine.
Look at her running as fast as a cheetah.
She has amazing eyes looking for prey.

Shannon Nicol (8)
Forehill Primary School, Ayr

Fred With The Big Head

His bright gloomy eyes looking straight at you for death.
Its grey shining horns glaring like the sun.
The sharp, blood-dripping teeth.
Sharp pointy scales as sharp as a knife.
Fast, fierce fire sparking away to death.

Xander Innes (7)
Forehill Primary School, Ayr

Slurper Slimer

Feel the slime from his ugly two shady blotches.
Hear the stamps, closer and closer.
Touch the infected skin that burns until you melt.
Smell the bogey brain with a lot of flavour.
See the sharp teeth that can snap.

Abigail Jopp (8)
Forehill Primary School, Ayr

Chubby Cokie

Look at his delicate headpiece that his granny gave him.
Hear the ripped jeans getting ripped even more.
Watch him run very quickly.
His gloomy feet shine in the sun.
Watch him fly through the bright, bright sky.

Oriana Thomson (8)
Forehill Primary School, Ayr

Milly Monster

Milly has teeth as sharp as knives.
She has three heads and that annoys her always.
Look at her big belly.
She has a lot of spots.
She eats kids.

Ellie Goudie (8)

Forehill Primary School, Ayr

Crazy Bobby Land

I saw a monster watching Candyland Band,
He even had some spicy crisps as big as milk
cartons in his hand.
Crazy Bobby is his crazy monster name,
He doesn't want anyone to be the same.
Crazy Bobby has a long nap lying on the carpet,
Before he goes to the very busy market.
The leader of Crazy Bobby Land will never sit still,
Well, because he always has an energy pill.
He has a bell with a red dot on it,
It rings when he jumps into his ball pit.
He eats blueberries that are very ripe,
He sucks them through a rusty downpipe.

Orla Nic Roibín (8)
Gaelscoil Léim An Mhadaidh, Limavady

The Swamp Monster

I see a slimy monster chomping in the swamp,
He looks like a hairy lump.
His head is as white as snow,
He is like a sloth because he is very slow.
He has lots of tiny feet,
In a race he's hard to beat.
He loves to eat raw fish,
Which is his favourite dish.
He is terrified of boys and girls,
He collects shiny pearls.
Boys and girls are scared of him too,
He likes to scare people by shouting, "Boo!"

Kiefer Lucas Ó Maoláin (8)
Gaelscoil Léim An Mhadaidh, Limavady

Ocean

Ocean is very friendly, cute and neat,
Ocean is very sweet,
Ocean's best friend is Aqua Gem,
Aqua Gem loves to use colourful pens.
Ocean has two pets called Gem and Pearl,
Ocean's pets are puppies and they are both girls,
Ocean only eats waffles, large and flat,
That's why she's so fat.
Plop! Oh no Gem and Pearl fell in the pool,
But Gem and Pearl thought it was pretty cool.

Ria Ní Earcáin (8)
Gaelscoil Léim An Mhadaidh, Limavady

Ginger Adventure

I still slide downstairs like I am on a slipping slide,
I glide through the kitchen when nobody's inside.
I sneakily come out of the attic,
Don't mind me, my spikes always go static!
I'm as cold as an ice cube, do you still like me?
My favourite thing to do is have a cup of tea.
I was trying very hard to make marshmallows,
Quick someone's coming I will have to hide behind the wheelbarrows.

Mollie Nic Giolla Comhaill (8)
Gaelscoil Léim An Mhadaidh, Limavady

The Rainbow Monster

Pearl the monster lived in a magical tree,
Pearl found a magical tiny rainbow baby bee.
Pearl is the most friendly monster in town,
Pearl found a massive slippy rainbow hill and slid down.
When the rainbow monster goes near light she looks like a pearl,
And she likes to pivot, twist and twirl.
She is as fluffy as a sheep,
And you'll find it tricky to wake her if she ever falls asleep.

Saorise Nic Amhalaí (7)
Gaelscoil Léim An Mhadaidh, Limavady

The Rainbow Monster

I found a monster under my bed,
It had purple fingers and her antenna was red.
Her name was Rainy, she was loving and kind,
I have to admit she was a really good find.
Rainy was lazy and spotty,
With big red dots all over her body.
She doesn't like it when she gets too spotty.
When we're gone she makes a mess in my room,
When I get back I hand her a broom.

Ava Grace Nic Hoirbín (8)
Gaelscoil Léim An Mhadaidh, Limavady

Crazy Spike On My Bike

I found a monster in my bed,
His horns were seeping out red.
I saw a monster on my bike,
His name is Crazy Spike.
He loves to eat sweets
Because it's a sugary treat.
He loves to eat food that's as white as snow,
Because it helps him grow.
He's as bouncy as a beach ball,
As spiky as holly.
He's always grumpy and he's never jolly.

Elin Ní Anderson (9)
Gaelscoil Léim An Mhadaidh, Limavady

Clawbone's Body

I am hungry and slimy like my big brother,
Who loves the way how our loving mother
takes care of us more than our very strong dad,
That gives us very gross meat and I think he's bad!

My name is Clawbone and I am so large,
I am the only monster in charge,
I am as slimy as putty and I am as slippery as a snake,
And when I roar the ground starts to shake!

Casey Ó Sabhain (7)
Gaelscoil Léim An Mhadaidh, Limavady

Pumpkin Patch

I found a monster under my bed,
He said his name was Father Ted.
He said he had a magic spell,
I was so shocked I almost fell.
He had tentacles as green as leaves
And when people smelt him everybody heaved.
He lived in a pumpkin patch
And his pumpkin kept running away.
He tried so hard to catch it
But when he did it would not stay.

Conor O Brolcháin (8)
Gaelscoil Léim An Mhadaidh, Limavady

The Teddy Bear Monster

My teddy lives under my chair,
One morning he wasn't there,
I saw him sneak into my sister's bedroom,
And I heard the biggest boom!
He broke my sister's vase and blamed it on me,
My sister heard the crash and wailed like a banshee
And she shouted at me and I started to weep,
Why was she so annoyed, that vase was very cheap!

Aliona Ní Mhaoláin (7)
Gaelscoil Léim An Mhadaidh, Limavady

Timmy

The monster creeps around my house all night,
But that sneaky monster stays out of sight.
One day when I opened the kitchen door,
He gave an almighty roar.

He always munches on blueberries,
He nearly threw up when he ate cherries.
I tried to take his photo and when he saw a flash,
He ran up the stairs as fast as he could dash.

Chloe Ní Mhuirí (9)
Gaelscoil Léim An Mhadaidh, Limavady

Jimbob Freaks

Jimbob likes to play hide-and-seek,
When he runs around the floorboards creak.
When people walk past he likes to shout, "Boo!"
Then the people cry, "Boo hoo hoo!"
He likes to give them quite a fright,
Especially in the middle of the night.
Jimbob is huge and hairy
And sometimes can be a little scary.

Braiden Ní Labhraí (9)
Gaelscoil Léim An Mhadaidh, Limavady

Rainbow Stripe

I saw a monster doing a flip,
When he landed on his lip,
I heard him creaking through the door,
Then he gave a mighty roar.
He was as colourful as a rainbow up in the sky,
And when he stood up he was nearly as high.
The only thing Rainbow Stripe likes to eat
Is the children he finds out on the street.

Riley Mag Aoidh (8)
Gaelscoil Léim An Mhadaidh, Limavady

The Giraffe Monster

I hear a monster in my attic,
I can imagine in my head his hair is very static.
His name is Slinky
And he is very stinky.
I heard a big munch,
I think he is eating my lunch.
He's nowhere to be seen,
I don't know where he has been.
When he is away
I hope he has an amazing day!

Aoife Nic Congail (9)
Gaelscoil Léim An Mhadaidh, Limavady

Elliot And Mr Slim

I heard a big loud snore,
I tried so hard but I couldn't ignore.
I saw a huge red head
And that's when I knew there was a monster in my bed!
He had a friend along with him,
A big tall bear called Mr Slim.
Mr Slim was not very nice,
So I ran away as quickly as scurrying mice.

Ellie-Mai de Craig (8)
Gaelscoil Léim An Mhadaidh, Limavady

The Shy Monster

One morning I was in my bed,
I heard a noise, it was a crash in the shed.
I saw a monster,
He was enormous, he was red with orange spots,
He was friendly but shy
And his spots looked like dots.
We ate some sweets,
I turned on the radio
And we listened to some funky beats.

Avril Ní Chárthaigh (7)
Gaelscoil Léim An Mhadaidh, Limavady

Daisy The Crazy Monster

I am fluffy like a puppy,
I am friendly too,
But you better watch out,
I can be as crazy as a zoo.
I am very cute and clever
And if you feel unwell,
My hugs will make you better,
It's just like a magic spell.

Yasmin Ní Mhaolaín (7)
Gaelscoil Léim An Mhadaidh, Limavady

Wiggler

I heard a bumping monster in my loo,
His body was as scaly
As the bottom of my shoe.
He gave me a fright
But then I giggled,
So you better watch out
Or you'll get wiggled!

Dara Mac Aoidh (9)
Gaelscoil Léim An Mhadaidh, Limavady

Fast Twinkles

I heard a monster under my bed,
Her name is Twinkles and she is all red.
She is friendly and likes to play,
She loves to dance night and day.

Brooke Ní Ghliasáin-Ní Ghabhann (7)
Gaelscoil Léim An Mhadaidh, Limavady

Dotty The Spotty Monster

My monster's name is Dotty
And she is really, very spotty.
Whenever she's in town she stops and dances around.
Dotty walks down the street nearly every single day,
Beware of Dotty the monster because she will chase you away!
When she shouts it means she's really mad,
and when she yelps, it means she is very sad.
Sometimes she runs up and down the street,
And she can sometimes be quite friendly to meet.
Only once or twice a day,
Dotty the monster might like to play.
When this petrifying monster is around,
She can get lost and not be found!
Dotty the monster is only scared of one thing,
She is scared of long pieces of string!
The only reason is because,
It gets stuck in-between her big orange paws!

Isabella Mitchell (8)
Old Sarum Primary School, Old Sarum

Flo The Monster

Ding-dong went the bell,
I opened the door to a horrific smell.
There stood a monster,
Big and blue,
I let it in and it found the loo.
I asked, "What is your name?"
I didn't know.
It replied, "My name is Flo."

The monster is big,
The monster is blue,
I really don't like it,
It smells of poo.

We went to bed,
I couldn't sleep,
My eyes watered,
I started to weep.

Elliot Smith (9)
Old Sarum Primary School, Old Sarum

The Snake-Like Pinnochio's Tail

My monster has an eerie tail,
Her name is Veronica.
In the early hours you can hear her playing the harmonica.
Every time she tells a tale an extra metre her tail will grow.
In the dead of night children beware, Veronica's tail flicks everywhere.
Don't go to sleep or she might creep and scare you in your sleep.
This concludes Veronica's tale.
Just be aware of her extraordinary tail.

Elly-Mae Willock (10)
Old Sarum Primary School, Old Sarum

The Demon In My Locker

Who's that guy at my school?
I look inside my locker and who do I see?
A three-headed demon looking at my wide eyes.
The thing climbed out of my locker and it chased me down the hallway.
It was breathing fire everywhere and the whole hall was being destroyed.
I ran into my classroom and I told my teacher.
She opened the doors and she said nothing was ever wrong!

Dylan Thomas Chandler (7)
Old Sarum Primary School, Old Sarum

He Is There...

When I woke up I felt refreshed,
but then I fell out of bed.
Then I saw these two, or should I say two and a half, eyes staring at me,
They had bloody veins running through them.
I jumped up with all my energy and ran.
I've been dreaming for weeks but when I play hide-and-seek
I think it looks cute but it tries to swallow me!

Aya Bendhiyaf (10)
Old Sarum Primary School, Old Sarum

A Monster Called Grumpy

There was a monster called Grumpy
Every day Grumpy was grumpy.
When Grumpy got older he started to get spots
He started to get snake-like.
He learned how to shape-shift.
He started to act like a real monster.
There was a monster called Grumpy
And Grumpy will always be grumpy.

Skye Thomas (9)
Old Sarum Primary School, Old Sarum

Big Monster

There was a big monster
As spooky as can be
Walking down the street
Looking for naughty children
For him to bring back home.

This is the scariest monster
Down the street.

Jasmine Pemberton (6)
Old Sarum Primary School, Old Sarum

Rainbow Drop

Here comes the rain
Hooray, hooray!
Splashing in the puddles
Hooray, hooray!
Here comes the sun
Hooray, hooray!
Rainbow Drop is here
Hooray, hooray!
Out to play!

Chloe Kimberly Baker (7)
Old Sarum Primary School, Old Sarum

Slimy The Happy Monster

Slimy has colourful legs.
When the sun shines his legs makes rainbows.
His wobbly eyes make people smile.
He dances crazily with colourful boots.
He is not scary, he is very funny.

Beau (6)
Old Sarum Primary School, Old Sarum

Funny Bones

Funny Bones is big and bright
He can see really well with his big eyes.
So prepare for a big surprise,
His teeth are big and like sharp knives
So make sure you run for your life!

Isabella Beauchamp (7)
Old Sarum Primary School, Old Sarum

The Loch Ness Monster

The slimy and gooey and giant monster
Once found a big park to scare people
But then he remembered what his teacher said
about being kind,
So he was always kind.

Jessica Davies (6)
Old Sarum Primary School, Old Sarum

Spark

S park is a storyteller,
P ast and future,
A dd some fun,
R evolting and picture-perfect,
K eep Spark secret please!

Eloise Kennedy (10)
Old Sarum Primary School, Old Sarum

What Would I Do?

If I had wings...
I would push the clouds away,
I would swish through the sky,
I would fish in the sea.

If I had talons...
I could shave the grass,
I could clutch a field of wheat,
I could dig through Mount Everest.

If I had a tail...
I would smash a vault and steal the gold,
I would wrap my tail tight around me,
I would scoop it up all the plastic in the ocean.

If I had razor-sharp teeth...
I would catch fish,
I would tear a school down.

If I had scales...
I would polish them,
I would slither like a snake,
I would shed my skin.

Patsy Griffiths (8), Alfie & Lucus Connolly (8)
St Bartholomew's CE Primary School, Stourport-On-Severn

Freddy The Frightening Dragon

Freddy the fiery, flaming dragon
who loves to fly up high in the beautiful blue sky.
He has to say bye to his friends at 6pm,
that's when he rests and he's at his best.
His best friend's name is Sam
and she likes to eat some delicious pink ham.
She is as beautiful as a sparkling sink
or a star in the sky.
When it is night-time Freddy's skin turns black
but when it's all sunny Freddy is really light and on fire.

Ben Ellis (9)
St Bartholomew's CE Primary School, Stourport-On-Severn

Dragons Are Dead

D ead dragons
R eal dragons which are like the sun
A live dragons which are as fierce as a bear
G one forever dragons
O val belly-shaped dragons
N o dragons
S orry dragons (not)

A re dragons dead?
R ed dragons
E vil dragons

D evil dragons
E ating dragons
A ll dragons are gone
D inner time dragons.

Finley Ashdown (8)
St Bartholomew's CE Primary School, Stourport-On-Severn

Dragon Mystery

If I had wings
I would swoop down to the buildings and crash into water and take some for my baby dragons.

If I had talons
I would eat cheese on the way to the nail shop.

If I had a tail
I would whip bad people.

If I had razor-sharp teeth
I would eat buildings and destroy all the trees.

If I had scales
I would pretend to be a handbag and steal their cash and never ever stop.

Melody Bryant (8)
St Bartholomew's CE Primary School, Stourport-On-Severn

Dark Flyer

If I had wings
I would swoop and swing
Like a person in the ring
Dragons are non-fiction things
So if you are a Viking or are hiking
Just remember this...
If I had talons
I would go around the world before I'm told.
When you fly around the world
You must get ready so I'm not cold.

In the night it's clearly green,
His eyes are red as fire.

Yazmin Newton (8)
St Bartholomew's CE Primary School, Stourport-On-Severn

If I Had...

If I had wings
I'd swoop over the treetops.

If I had claws like blades
I'd eat yummy little souls super quick I think.

If I had razor-sharp teeth
I'd eat lots of raw meat by ripping it apart.

If I had a long, strong, stripy tail
I'd whip people into shape.

If I was a dragon
I'd put up a show in the sensational sky.

Macie Crumpton (8)
St Bartholomew's CE Primary School, Stourport-On-Severn

Cherry The Reddy

Cherry absolutely loves berries
And loves her mom, Clemmie.
She loves division
But has very bad vision.
Cherry is a rainbow across the sky
And she goes to buy a bunch of berries for lunch.
Cherry the sinister dragon was creeping towards the sweets
So her mom won't know what she eats.
She carefully creeps back to her room
To eat the sensational sour sweets!

Adriana Gabalaite (8)
St Bartholomew's CE Primary School, Stourport-On-Severn

The Magnificent Dragon

If I had a treacherous, tall tail
I would whip the world into shape.

If I had a treacherous, tall tail
I would strike all the people who are bad.

If I had wild, wonderful wings
I'd fly into the magnificent forest and save the Minpins.

If I had wild, wondrous wings
I'd fly over snowy mountains and fizzing hot volcanoes.

Katelyn Mason (9)
St Bartholomew's CE Primary School, Stourport-On-Severn

Bob The Dragon

He is the strongest, most fierce dragon,
Although he is so clumsy you know,
He climbs up trees then falls out them,
Clumsily onto his knees.
He used to flee by climbing up trees
But he didn't because he's Bob,
Bob the dragon.
Yes! Bob the dragon
That falls out of trees onto his knees
And sometimes gets fleas.

Olly Kendrick (8)
St Bartholomew's CE Primary School, Stourport-On-Severn

Death The Dragon

D eath the dangerous, dirty dragon was
R oaring fiercely for revenge.
A ttack! he thought. He wanted to feast for the blood so he
G reedily watched the Vikings whilst they were hiking
O n the icy, slippery mountain
N obody could see him lurking so he swooped on down, ate a human and began burping.

Isabelle (8)
St Bartholomew's CE Primary School, Stourport-On-Severn

If I Had...

If I had wings
I'd fly to America to see Donald Trump.

If I had talons
I'd climb to the top of Mount Everest.

If I had a tail
I'd whip the Russians!

If I had razor-sharp teeth
I'd eat chewy meat.

If I had scales
I'd be a handbag.

Ollie Howard Curzey (8)
St Bartholomew's CE Primary School, Stourport-On-Severn

Annie The Awesome Dragon

Annie was lurking like an animal about to catch her prey.
She lives in the ice-cold glacier day by day
Annie the Awesome dragon likes eating Vikings that go hiking.
Annie has magical wings,
She goes to ring the bell that dings!
And there's nothing she loves
More than her mom called Bing.

Olivia Mitchell (9)
St Bartholomew's CE Primary School, Stourport-On-Severn

Dark Side

If I had wings
I'd save the world.

If I had talons
I would scratch then tear apart.

If I had a tail
I would sweep the whole world tidy.

If I had razor-sharp teeth
I would eat everything in the world.

If I had scales
I wouldn't hurt my back.

Laytton Loveridge (8)
St Bartholomew's CE Primary School, Stourport-On-Severn

Death The Almighty Dragon

My dragon is cute, that's what I think.
But others disagree because they say he stinks.
His name is Death and he has awful breath.
He is very black and he has gigantic spikes on his back.
He has almighty strength and could lift two trucks
He got all his tricks from his magic book.

Lacey May Webb (8)
St Bartholomew's CE Primary School, Stourport-On-Severn

Gloopy The Monster

If I had wings
I would swoop around the tallest trees.
If I had talons
I would slice a pizza box in half.
If I had a tail
I would use it as a weapon.
If I had razor-sharp teeth
I could eat lots of chewing gum.
If I had scales
I would shine in the light of the sun.

Liberty Middleton (8)
St Bartholomew's CE Primary School, Stourport-On-Severn

Robin The Magnificent

Robin the magnificent is like a multicoloured rainbow.
He sparkles in the sky,
Swooping like a butterfly.
Although he's shy he's a devil in the sky.
He is my favourite pet
But he hates seeing the vet.
He hugs me like a teddy bear,
Keeping me safe, always be aware.

Phoebe Southwick (8)
St Bartholomew's CE Primary School, Stourport-On-Severn

My Sky Dragon

She loves flying so high,
She goes into the fluffy clouds in the sky.
She flies close to the sun
Which is a flaming hot volcano.
She is like a firework shooting across the sky,
She is a dragon, not just any dragon,
A super high-flying, almighty dragon.

Sophie Holly Webb (8)
St Bartholomew's CE Primary School, Stourport-On-Severn

A Dragon To Love

D ragons are dirty liars
R eal to love, fake to kill
A re they? Yes, I have one dragon he is Galaxy
and he has golden wings.
G ood, well-behaved dragon
O nly one type I love
N ever break friendships.

Mia Grace Jones (8)
St Bartholomew's CE Primary School, Stourport-On-Severn

Your Death

The dangerous dragon drives in a car.
He likes to eat human souls.
He has wings like an eagle.
He has razor-sharp teeth.
He loves to eat children,
Especially brainy children.
He is like the opposite of the world's guardian.

Faustas Augys (8)
St Bartholomew's CE Primary School, Stourport-On-Severn

The Dragon Poem

A dragon is as fierce as a roasting fire.
A dragon likes to eat fresh mountains of meat.
A dragon flies like a meteor out of the sky.
He crashes down hard into the Earth nearby.
A dragon has camouflage, scales and almighty
sharp tail.

Elliot Taylor (8)
St Bartholomew's CE Primary School, Stourport-On-Severn

Dragons

D eplorable dragons,
R oaring and snoring,
A doringly sleeping,
G roaning and thumping
O n his hay bed,
N ot liking Vikings,
S narling secretly in the dark cold night.

Autumn Joy Birch (8)
St Bartholomew's CE Primary School, Stourport-On-Severn

Sparkle

Sparkle is wild.
Sparkle is dusty.
Sparkle is ferocious.
Sparkle does not stop eating fish.
Sparkle is a loving pet.
My dragon is like my BFF.
My dragon will never go away.

Jazmin Bower (8)
St Bartholomew's CE Primary School, Stourport-On-Severn

The Very Hungry Monster

Claws gripping to the ivy as she crawls up the wall in the dead of night,
Softly, slowly, creeping quietly out of sight.
Easing open the window, creeping under the bed,
Rubbing her tummy, thinking, *it's time for me to be fed.*
Five eyes blinking, looking around in fright,
Trying really hard to stay out of sight.
Suddenly, I wake up and see her standing there,
A cute and fluffy monster looking around in despair.
I say to the monster, "What's wrong?"
And he sits upon my chair.
"I have travelled far and wide," she said,
"To find someone who will talk to me
And now I see it's true!
My friends always said there are nice people with lots of lovely food."
Then I said to the monster,
"Well, it's your lucky day, we have so much food in our fridge,

Let's go without delay."
So me and the little monster went downstairs.

Abigail Bartle (7)
St Martin's CE (VA) Primary School, Fangfoss

Princess Poppy's Life

P ocklington in The Lilacs,
R iding on my bike.
I n a corner looking scared,
N ot knowing I was there,
C ute, fluffy and wearing a pink dress.
E asily decided to tell Mummy and Daddy.
S o Mummy said, "Invite her in."
"S he's a monster though Mummy!"

P rincess Poppy is very helpful and loving.
O n school days she plays with Mummy.
P oppy tidies my room even if I don't ask her to.
P ie is this monster's favourite food.
Y es! She is my new friend.

Esme Thomas (7)
St Martin's CE (VA) Primary School, Fangfoss

The Terror Hammer!

The armored monster has an electrifying tail and a massive hammer.
He has a big roar and he smells of mouldy cheese.
He has a lot of blood on his hammer.
He looks like a big spiky rock,
Well, that's what I read in the monster manual,
But then I let him out of the cage.
When I opened the cage door he ran out and jumped on the sofa
And literally wrecked the place,
So I took him outside then he ran off and I ran after him.
After a while I caught him and named him Terror Hammer!
So I took him home and put him to bed.

Archie Sissons (8)
St Martin's CE (VA) Primary School, Fangfoss

Monsters

My monster is called Gloop the hairy giant,
He is addicted to coffee with toffee,
He is about six foot two,
When he's tired he looks like a big sloth,
His hobby is killing gnats,
To make an excuse for taking a bath,
His bloodshot eyes give people a fright,
So they hurry and scurry back to their mummy,
Be careful or you will be stumbling on his stubble,
I love my monster, but if you get too close
Get ready to smell gross.

Emma Rebecca Curtis (8)
St Martin's CE (VA) Primary School, Fangfoss

Mr Hairy Feet, Bob

He's got hairy feet but he can dance to a beat.
He's crazy when he's lazy but he is unknown.
He smells like cheese after he's jumped on the sofa.
He burps and he slurps after he's had a drink.
He may sound crazy but he does have normal showers.
He runs around the street kissing his feet.
My monster was dug up by my mum.
He may poo his pants when he hasn't got a chance!

Oliver Eden Harrison (7)
St Martin's CE (VA) Primary School, Fangfoss

Shadow King Showdown

S hadow King lives in the wardrobe
H iding under the bed
A lways there at night
D id you see him in the darkness?
O ne large black cape
W hiffing of mystery

K ing of the night-time monsters
I am scared he might come and get me
N ight light kept on then safe from Shadow King
G oing to sleep now - night-night!

William Alexander Brack (7)
St Martin's CE (VA) Primary School, Fangfoss

My Monster Poem

There was a monster on my street
Eating some ding-dong bells
He had a slimy head and dirty feet
He knocked on the door
My mum said to the monster to come.
He was quite big, twenty-three metres long.
My mum had lots of traps in the garden
That's because he's not allowed in the garden
My mum trapped him in the trap
But he ran to the next-door neighbour.

Kuba Cierniak (7)
St Martin's CE (VA) Primary School, Fangfoss

Love Heart Monster

She is big and she is funny
I am tired and she will never ever go to bed
She is crazy, she's just lovely
She smells beautiful like roses

Her name is Snowy and she is very happy
She looks very cute and was love heart eyes.
She has bright pink hair and a spiky tail
Which has colourful stripes.

She is the love heart monster.

Lotty Harrison (7)
St Martin's CE (VA) Primary School, Fangfoss

You Don't Want To Put Up A Fight On The Night

She might be cheeky
But at the same time she might be greedy.
She'll wait and have to count to one, two, three
When we are having tea.
You and me will be shamed and framed
And it might have to be tamed.
I am very sad because my furniture and glass is broken
Which I have chosen.
She isn't very smart because she ate a jam tart.

Evelyn May Anne Baxter (7)
St Martin's CE (VA) Primary School, Fangfoss

Monster Ponster

My monster is ugly, he looks all square
Some people might think he's really a bear.

He's sneaky, quiet and sly,
But he's unable to fly.

He's really rather scary
But his name isn't Mary.

Sometimes he's annoying
So you're usually best avoiding.

Daniel Bell (7)
St Martin's CE (VA) Primary School, Fangfoss

Blobby Is Knobbly

Blobby is knobbly
He eats whatever he sees.
And his favourite food is keys.
He likes to play with the dog and so don't forget to knock.
Because the door might be locked.
He has horns with fire on them
And six scary eyes which keep a lookout for tasty key pies to eat.

Henry Thomas Duncan (7)
St Martin's CE (VA) Primary School, Fangfoss

Giggles

G iggles is a loving thing
I think he's caring and fluffy as a teddy
G iggles is not a human, he's a monster
G iggles loves to roar
L ove the roaring, I do
E lsa does (me)
S omeone or something is creeping around!

Elsa Grace Rogers (7)
St Martin's CE (VA) Primary School, Fangfoss

A Boy That Has A Monster

There was a monster called Jons who was good at flying.
He was a monster that could fly like mad
And he spent it eating insects like flies and woodlice,
Also dogs, cats and little children.
He stayed up for two days
And then slept for two days.

Tom Lee (7)
St Martin's CE (VA) Primary School, Fangfoss

Monster

M ean
O range and black
N aughty
S cary
T errifying
E ats piglets
R oars a lot.

Courtney G (8)
St Martin's CE (VA) Primary School, Fangfoss

The Creeping Monster

Meet Creeping, she is as creepy as a killer
Running across the street
In the middle of the night screaming,
"I'm arrested! I'm arrested!"
Her claws are as sharp as a cactus.
Her hair is as tall as Mount Olympus!
She loves eating boys, especially naughty ones!
She's like a vampire but with way sharper teeth.
She's even a demon and in Hell.
Well, I wouldn't say in real Hell, I mean fake!
So I built it for Creeping.
The only annoying bit is... food!
I have to give it to her when she falls asleep...
Now here's the really good part and bad part...
Good is first...
She is pretty nice and always keeping an eye.
Bad... She never eats her food but eats books!
I think that's all you need to know!

Susan Turley (7)
Wilshere Dacre Junior Academy, Hitchin

A Scary Poem To Make You Shiver

There is a monster called Twinkle,
She is pretty and not very mean,
But the only way to make her angry
Is to wind her up and you don't want to do that
Because she really will be mean,
She is a lady,
She has everything in the world you could ask for,
She is very fast.
"There's a monster in the village,"
Everybody shouts, "Help!"
Twinkle says, "Don't worry, I'm not going to eat you."
Everybody sighs in relief,
They all make friends
And have a jolly drink.
So if you have a monster problem
Just say, "I'm not scared
And do you want to come and play?"
"Let's have some fun," said Twinkle.
You may not believe this is true

But Twinkle is a beautiful young monster,
She is eight years old.
Twinkle is beautiful,
She has a boyfriend called Spiky
And he is ten years old.
She loves him very much,
They go for ice cream every day.

Olivia Matthews (7)
Wilshere Dacre Junior Academy, Hitchin

Tiny

Hello, I am Tiny and I am very kind and happy.
I am very quiet and very helpful and cheerful.
I am very red and tiny
And have one big eye in the middle of my head.
I have very sticky pads all over me like an octopus.
I have very short hair which is curly.
I only have one tooth.
I have a very kind neighbour who likes my long, long tail which hasn't got sharp lumps on it which is basically what everybody likes.
I always persevere, cheer my friends up like a normal person would do to help them.
I am very gentle and a tiny bit naughty but push that bit out of your head because I have got something even more interesting for you.
A secret I have never told anyone!
I live under a bed.

Emma Whiting (8)
Wilshere Dacre Junior Academy, Hitchin

Monster Power

My monster may be powerful but can't knock down a tree
But knocked down people did he.
He would stamp down his tail knocking everything in sight,
But make earthquakes he might.
Who has met a monster nine feet tall
But wouldn't eat an animal?
No never, he would only eat people!
His favourite food is Minotaurs!
He is always looking for s'mores!
He is very lucky but can be very plucky
But nobody knows why he's so lucky!
So he will never ever call himself a big baby
But his tail is so big
Though he doesn't look like a pig.
He says. "Destroy humans, I'm big!"
And his blood cells are enormous!

Joshua Morgan (7)
Wilshere Dacre Junior Academy, Hitchin

Squiglet Really Loves To Draw

Squiglet really loves to draw
And she never eats any more!
When she draws in a line,
All her pictures come to life!
When they talk in such a fizz,
She'll help whatever their problem is,
But she never goes to the loos
And she never wears any shoes.
Squiglet never makes a mess,
She also never wears clothes or a dress
And she never wears a hood
But she's also very good.
I think she draws numbers too,
Come over here and I'll tell you.
She can also talk and sing
And crayons on a pad that she can bring.
She makes lots of friends as I can tell,
Probably you're her friend as you know her well!

Laya Mae Green (7)
Wilshere Dacre Junior Academy, Hitchin

The Electric Shot Monster

Hello, this is Electric Shot,
He is as fast as a cheetah,
If someones tries to get him he can fly, run, climb and be invisible.
He's as hungry as a ravenous lion.
He looks like a shark, leopard, gecko and a dragon.
He's as gentle as a soft cushion.
He really doesn't eat people but he eats animals.
My monster is revivable because he can revive.
My monster has sticky pads so if his wings broke he could stick to walls.
He has more six packs than anyone because he's got a twenty pack.
He roams through the eerie night waiting for children's s'mores.
If you take a peek he will end up torturing you in his jaws.

Lucas Young (7)
Wilshere Dacre Junior Academy, Hitchin

Zienna

She is as fluffy as a monkey
And as gentle as a fish.
She is fierce but cute.
Her horns are as short as a snake's tail.
She is a bit hairy
And a bit spotty.
She is a bit cheeky but still cute.
She is fast, naughty and a bit silly.
She is as short as a cat
And as hungry as a mouse.
She makes a big roar when people or other monsters are mean to her.
She smells as fresh as a whale does.
She's friendly like a barking puppy.
She is not mean, just a bit cheeky.
She's spotty and good,
She is never mean or bad.
There is just one thing,
She has no friends, she's lonely.

India-Mae Noone (7)
Wilshere Dacre Junior Academy, Hitchin

The Slimy Slug

Slimy is like a slug
But he has one eye,
His eye is blue.
His colour gives away where he lives,
The vines fall down on him,
He lives in a jungle,
He's slimy
And is as stinky as can be.
He lives by the sea,
Green slime oozes from him
But he always finds time to munch on his leaves.
He slithers in the swamp to go to bed,
Every morning he rises to the surface to have breakfast,
He slithered and slimed to find his way to his friend's home,
Trundling along in his slow time,
The only noise he makes is a slow grunting sound,
The swamp water burns against his side.

Elizabeth Dennis (7)
Wilshere Dacre Junior Academy, Hitchin

The Night Creak

He wanders through the night scaring you out of your bed,
He scares your dreams out of your head,
His horns sizzle like a sausage
And his favourite word is 'bobbage'.
If you are kind he will help you.
If you are not he will go boo-hoo.
Kindness is his favourite thing.
Listen to the train go ding-ding.
He howls like a wolf.
When everyone sees him they all go *balf*.
He wants to be a rockstar
But instead, he is a pop star.
All his friends are dead
But one sleeps inside his head.
If you ask him what's your name?
All he will answer is about his fame.

Eva Winstanley (7)
Wilshere Dacre Junior Academy, Hitchin

Max The Monster

Max is as funny as a bunny.
Max can play the Flute, ahh, that's so cute.
You cannot imagine how hungry he is,
He's extremely hungry.
He has no tail that leaves a trail.
He is not that hairy or that scary
But he is very small.
Max was in bed, turning his head left and right,
Then turned on the light
But there was nothing in sight.
Sometimes he can break the law
And scratch other monsters with his mighty claws.
Max is small, not very tall.
He can be naughty and a bit snorey
But I will always love my little monster
And he will always love me.

Myla Rose Gorski-Eaton (7)
Wilshere Dacre Junior Academy, Hitchin

Monsters

Some monsters are scary
And some of them are hairy.
Most of them drool
And some jump into slime pools.
Some monsters are old
And some of them are cold.
Some live underground,
Some don't stay in one place, they move around.
Some are so slimy they get stuck on walls,
Some are so friendly, they go to the mall.
Don't you see some monsters like you and me?
Even though they look creepy
They sometimes get very sleepy.
Some make a noise
But some really like to play with cute toys.
Some like to go on a swing
And some just go ping!

Sophie Jeffrey (8)
Wilshere Dacre Junior Academy, Hitchin

The Magic Lacey

The ferocious monster with a scaly back
Has ten hands, ten feet and carries a sack
She looks so pretty.
She is my love heart.
She is beautiful.
She's my apple tart,
She eats ten of them a day.
To keep her hunger away
If she is blinded the ten apples replace her eyes.
She likes spaghetti and loves eating fireflies
She's got unicorn horns
Her teeth are really sharp
She's got a garden at the back of her house
Where she plays the harp
She's got a swing, that's very big.
And while she is on it, she sleeps with a twig.

Gabrielle Bernice Odiana (7)
Wilshere Dacre Junior Academy, Hitchin

The Legendary Spikes

Spikes is as cuddly as a teddy bear when his spikes go away.
He is so spiky he can kill people if Spikes has his pointy spikes on.
Since this amazing, fantastic monster is so strong he can lift anything that comes his way.
But before Spikes is all perfect, he has to change his smell.
He is as smelly as socks from the first day of Earth which have never been cleaned.
When his dear friends come, his spikes go into mist.
Spikes is as fierce as fire.
One more thing, Spikes' enemies get ready for the worst battle of your life!
Roar!

Harveer Singh Nijjar (7)
Wilshere Dacre Junior Academy, Hitchin

Scary Beary

My monster needs a shave
And while he is shaving he is bathing.
My monster once jumped into a pool,
He thought the pool was pretty cool.
My monster has smelly feet,
My monster is also a cheat.
When he is a bad boy,
He is a sad boy.
But my monster likes school,
And sometimes he plays the fool.
His favourite friend is Bob.
Bob has a job.
When my monster feels a hunger,
He eats a burger.
He goes to monster school,
They have a colossal swimming pool.
My monster is one *very* brilliant ghoul.

Ben Evans (7)
Wilshere Dacre Junior Academy, Hitchin

Horns The Man-Eater

Horns, Horns, where is Horns?
Beware of Horns.
Horns the man-eater is nearby everyone,
The terrifying Horns,
He's attacking a village near my house,
He's made all the villagers go crazy
And now my house is on fire
And I'm poor now.
I only have one pound in my pocket,
Only one pound.
Life is so boring with Horns around,
Go Horns, please go, please Horns the man-eater,
The terrifying Horns is so scary,
Please help us, someone please help,
Horns is nearby,
Horns, the terrifying Horns.

James Hull (8)
Wilshere Dacre Junior Academy, Hitchin

My Monster

Dark, dark in the night
A monster comes to frighten.
My monster is cute, funny, weird, unusual
And it's definitely funky.
It likes to dance, it sometimes goes missing,
It sometimes falls asleep on the monsters' bench.
It's mysterious,
Sometimes it can turn into a hideous monster.
Sometimes it can turn so excited it explodes
And then on the wall, there are big blobs.
Sometimes it gets lonely, then sad.
When it's bored it goes on the monster trampoline
And this is my monster.

Keira Robinson (7)
Wilshere Dacre Junior Academy, Hitchin

The Big Hammerhead Beast

My monster is crazy,
He flies around every day,
He breathes like a dragon going everywhere,
Flying around a castle,
A forest,
A palace
And the world,
In space,
Until he's out of breath.
The next day he decided to run,
So he did the same thing,
Round the castle,
Through the forest,
In the palace,
Around the world.
He went to bed
And then he was jumping over the castle,
Over the forest,
Over the palace,

Around the world,
In space,
He went to bed.

Jackson Donnelly (8)
Wilshere Dacre Junior Academy, Hitchin

Monsters

Have you seen a monster before?
Monsters are as slimy as a slime ball
And some even drop slime balls.
Some are as dry as a snake that's been lying in the sun for twenty-four hours.
Some live underground and some don't.
Monsters jump into slime pools
And some jump into normal pools.
Then they're all slimy and some are clean.
If you wake up in the middle of the night a group of monsters will come and take you away.
Some monsters like to play and some don't.

Leonardo Dainton-Cadona (7)
Wilshere Dacre Junior Academy, Hitchin

The Wild Monster

I went in my room with a bit of gloom,
Seeing it was covered in goo.
I looked left and right,
Seeing there was nothing in sight.
But then I saw a thing
With its hands up dancing in the wind.
I let it in.
It got slime everywhere.
I was regretting that mistake so I had to escape.
One hour later, I thought it was gone,
But nope, it was still there.
There was slime everywhere, rainbow slime, lots of it.
It was in my hair.
Was it me or was I dreaming?

Emma Fenwick (7)
Wilshere Dacre Junior Academy, Hitchin

The Stealth King

Prowling around catching birds and monkeys,
It might even catch a donkey,
For it is the king of stealth,
Its fur is as camouflaged as a chameleon's skin,
It has a very powerful shin,
It even uses a bin,
Climbing through the undergrowth as stealthily as a snow leopard,
Trying and keeping out of sight,
Beware if it's lurking about,
Its sharp tail can slice through a tree,
But be warned of its front because it can split into three.

Max Folbigg (7)
Wilshere Dacre Junior Academy, Hitchin

The Monster Who Wouldn't Share

Once there was a monster who wouldn't share.
She scoffed her sandwiches, took her toys away,
Nothing could stop her from taking it away.
She said, "That's mine!" and, "Stop!"
One day she found herself with no dolls,
No food, no toys,
Everything had gone away.
She asked her friends if she could share
And they said, "Yes!"
That is how she learned to share,
So next time you have nothing, just ask.

Anne Coles Barrett (7)
Wilshere Dacre Junior Academy, Hitchin

Gentle Baby Toothless

The dragons fire or kill,
The babies are silly because they can't fly,
Baby Toothless is brave and can fly,
All dragons fire or kill.
Baby Toothless can fire fireballs at people,
Which are as loud as lightning crashing to the ground,
Dragons are gentle, only if you are bad the dragons fire or kill.
Baby Toothless is gentle because he won't bite or fight you.
Baby Toothless and the dragons can fly because they have beautiful wings.

Imogen Stubbs (8)
Wilshere Dacre Junior Academy, Hitchin

Kreapzapa

He comes out of his grave when you're sleeping,
He has a Vibranium sword and metal shield,
He can turn invisible,
And can scare you half to death if you look at him.
His favourite treat is children,
He thinks kids are delish,
He can defeat 10,000 armies in about two hours,
He has horns with venomous tips,
He can run at about 1,000 miles per hour,
He has big red eyes,
He can shape-shift.

Stanley Buckland (7)
Wilshere Dacre Junior Academy, Hitchin

Dread Walker

The dreadful beast walks east to find its prey,
It roars loud and it's very proud
When it devours a great white with all its might.
It will fight anything with its blood-red horns,
It tears through thorns to kill an animal,
Terrifying, it wants to see you dying.
Now it's eating, chomping, stomping,
Lasers come out of its gun,
He thinks it's very fun.

Jack Cummins (7)
Wilshere Dacre Junior Academy, Hitchin

Toppling Heads

My monster knocked a tree.
He looked like he needed a wee!
As he climbed up the tree,
He pulled off his top
And ripped off his trousers
As he gobbled up the leaves like a baboon.
He spun and fell on the floor
Like a dead bat toppling over.
He was as red as pants,
All his little heads were crossed.
Then his little heads crashed to the floor.

Flynn Jenkinson (7)
Wilshere Dacre Junior Academy, Hitchin

Scary Nat

He went out of the grave
And he walked all day.
He went back to the grave
And woke up the next day.
He woke very early,
Then he went in the big fat pool.
Let's hear some more...
My monster is as weird as a clown
And he even looks like a clown, a funny clown.
He needs to be a funny clown.
I woke up!

Fawzia Quddus (8)
Wilshere Dacre Junior Academy, Hitchin

What We Do Together

When we play hide-and-seek he sometimes wins
because he hides in a cloud or in another country.
When he flies he leaves a trail of buzzes that lasts
for an hour.
He can turn things to stone, which is as cold and
as slippery as ice but as solid as lots of different
types of metal.
When we play catch he sometimes turns the ball to
stone.

Edward Salmond (7)
Wilshere Dacre Junior Academy, Hitchin

Bony

Bony is a small, friendly dragon,
She is very cute and friendly, fun too.
She plays with her toys.
She loves to run in the neighbourhood
And sleep in my bed.
She has sharp teeth.
She shines in the dark and glistens and sparkles.
She shakes and cracks her wings when she flies in the sky up high.

Sophia Scheepers (7)
Wilshere Dacre Junior Academy, Hitchin

Barney The Dinosaur

He's eerie and he's dark
But loving and caring.
He sometimes protects you
But he sometimes doesn't.
He sneaks into your house
And eats all your food.
He can gobble up your meat inside your body in one gulp.
He's as tall as a big tree
And can camouflage as good as a snake.

Jonah Blue (7)
Wilshere Dacre Junior Academy, Hitchin

Naughty Nibble

Naughty Nibble is cheeky and dribbles.
She likes drinking monster dribble.
I know it's disgusting but it's only a name for a monster drink.
She likes eating monster mash,
It's a type of monster food
And it's very popular for monsters.
Naughty Nibble is a kind and caring monster.

Ellie-May Needham (8)
Wilshere Dacre Junior Academy, Hitchin

Crunch

His name is Crunch.
He loves to munch.
He's taller than a crane.
He's stronger than a lion's mane.
He's ready to smash.
He makes cars crash.
He hates dice
So he splashes them with mice.
He's taller than thirty meteors,
He's tough like some creatures.

Joshua Jeeves (7)
Wilshere Dacre Junior Academy, Hitchin

Fluffy

Her name is Fluffy,
She is as cute as a puppy.
Fluffy is as joyful as an acrobat,
She's as cuddly as a teddy bear.
Fluffy is as funny as a clown.
Her horns are as pointy as a crocodile's teeth.
Her eyes sparkle like a full moon at night.
Her bow is as pretty as a flower.

Eva Carelli
Wilshere Dacre Junior Academy, Hitchin

Pac-Man

Pac-Man is as tall as Big Ben.
With a flick, he will send you to space at 61mph.
He is as yellow as the sun.
He is as hungry as a thousand sharks.
When he jumps the ground goes *crumble!*
But inside he is a very lonely giant with no friends.
Will you be his friend?

Ronnie Harris-Dawes (7)
Wilshere Dacre Junior Academy, Hitchin

River The Monster

Hi, I'm a monster who is kind
And makes you happy and safe.
My name is River and I am five
And I have long sharp fangs.
Today is my birthday
And I'm having a sleepover.
Two of my friends' names are Ava and Connor,
They are camping in my back garden.

Erin Hart (8)
Wilshere Dacre Junior Academy, Hitchin

Bamodom

My monster is silly,
He likes exciting lilies.
He moves so quickly
And he's so smiley.
I'll give you some silly examples,
One, he baths every day naked.
Two, he brushes his teeth with tape.
Three, he has a sofa made out of snowflakes.

Isabella Evans (7)
Wilshere Dacre Junior Academy, Hitchin

Deadly Raptor

Deadly Raptor saw a pig
And wanted to catch it.
Deadly Raptor was as big as a mansion.
He had claws as sharp as a knife
And his mouth had teeth like a shark.
Deadly Raptor liked to swim
But he liked to look in bins.

Luca William Jones (8)
Wilshere Dacre Junior Academy, Hitchin

Jeff, The Vicious Monster

I thought I saw a monster
Underneath my bed
With a very big head.

I thought I saw a monster
Underneath my pillow,
I thought I saw a monster
Looking through my window.

I thought I saw a monster
In my room last night.
There was a big boom,
It gave me a fright.

Dion Connah (10)
Ysgol Brynaerau, Pontllyfni

Bob The Monster

I saw a monster,
It gave me a fright.
I ran to my bed
Late at night.

Frightened and alone
I wished to turn on the light
But would I dare?
It might be a terrifying sight.

I did,
I hoped it would not bite.
I turned on the light
But the creature wasn't in sight!

I searched the house
Because I didn't feel safe at night.
In the bathroom, there was a noise
That gave me such a fright.

Out he came
With tissue paper on his foot.

The monster was made of tar,
Why was he barefoot?

It had one eye, red as blood
And super bright like a flashlight.
He was fatter than an elephant,
The door was too tight.

I cried for help,
The monster fled,
Alone,
I sat on my bed.

Then I saw the gruesome monster
Which now I call... Bob!
He's now my friend
And he gave me a job.

We played all night
When we should be asleep
Like tag and hide-and-seek
But he'll always peep!

I have to go to school though
So he hides in my bag.

We would have so much fun
Playing a game of tag.

If my mum heard this,
She would pass out
And Dad would shout,
"Get it out!"

Alisha Leigh Becker (11)
Ysgol Brynaerau, Pontllyfni

Bob's Adventure

I thought I saw a monster
In my room at night.
I called him Bob
And he liked corn on the cob.

He started throwing stuff
All over the room
And then I thought
I was in doom!

He went outside as fast as a cat
I looked through the peephole
And I saw...
Him climbing a pole.

He went *boom!*
On the floor
And then he started running
Towards the door.

I blocked the door
To stop the deadly guy.

"Please leave me alone,
I don't want to die."

Hari Carroll (8)
Ysgol Brynaerau, Pontllyfni

The Friendly Monster

I thought I heard a monster
Rummaging through the bins
Throwing the rubbish around
Most were tins.

I thought I saw a monster
In my house
He looked at me
He was as quiet as a mouse.

I thought I heard a monster
Opening the front door
Then eating everything
I hid on the floor.

I saw the monster
He was in my room
I was under my sheets shaking
And then he shouted, "Boom!"

I talked to the monster
I called him Billy

And took him downstairs
He was a friendly one.

Tomi Williams (10)
Ysgol Brynaerau, Pontllyfni

Noodles The Monster

I thought I saw a monster
Underneath my bed
He gobbled me up
And I thought I was dead.

I thought I saw a monster
Underneath my chair
And then I was screaming, "Where? Where?"
And then I went over there.

I thought I saw a monster
Looking through my window.
He could limbo
Under a bungalow.

I thought I saw a monster
In my room last night.
He grumbled and rumbled,
It gave me a fright.

I thought I saw a monster
And that he saw me...

And then I screamed,
"OMG!"

Elisha Hayes (11)
Ysgol Brynaerau, Pontllyfni

Stinky The Monster

I thought I saw a monster
Underneath my bed
He was very stinky
Eating a head.

I thought I saw a monster
Underneath my chair
Eating lots of chocolate
Like a wild bear.

I thought I heard a monster
Bursting down my door
Bang, bang, bang
And screaming, "Roar!"

I thought I smelt a monster,
He was very, very stinky.
I wanted to faint,
It wasn't very funky.

I thought I touched a monster,
He was really fluffy.

I was petrified
And I shouted, "Help me!"

Celt Pritchard-Jones (9)
Ysgol Brynaerau, Pontllyfni

Monster Mine

I thought I saw a shadow
Underneath my seat
I didn't know what to do
So I went into the street.

I'm sure I heard a monster in my wardrobe
Snoring away
I was scared
And I went very grey.

I saw something big,
It looked very ugly
I was scared to death
But so, so snuggly.

I heard something loud
Like a trumpet
What was it?
Doesn't matter, I want a crumpet.

I thought I smelt a monster
In the kitchen, eating food

I didn't know what was happening
But he was kinda rude...

Jarno Burgess (10)
Ysgol Brynaerau, Pontllyfni

Nutella The Fishy Monster

I thought I saw a scary monster
Underneath my bed.
He was very hairy
Like my head.

I thought I saw a giant monster
Underneath my chair.
Then he zoomed through the hallway
While eating a pear.

I thought I saw a deadly monster
In my closet.
I checked it out,
He was in my pocket.

I thought I saw a funny monster
Hiding behind the door.
I tried to squeeze him there,
Then he shouted, "Roar!"

I thought I saw a fat monster
And that he saw me.

I wanted to scream,
"Let me be!"

Osian Hywel Roberts (9)
Ysgol Brynaerau, Pontllyfni

Sneaky The Monster

I thought I saw a monster
Underneath my bed
He had red, disgusting eyes
And a gross, enormous head.

I thought I saw a monster
Underneath my chair
He was green like sick
And had purple hair.

I thought I saw a monster
Looking through my window
His tongue as sharp as a razor
I hid my head under my pillow.

I thought I saw a monster
In my room last night
And he was as bright as a light
He had a golden leg.

I thought I saw a monster
And that he saw me

I screamed and shouted,
"Let me be!"

Bethany Whitear (8)
Ysgol Brynaerau, Pontllyfni

Mandy The Malicious Monster

I thought I saw a monster
In my little backyard
He looked a little weird
Sitting and writing a card.

I thought I heard a monster
Going *whoosh, swish, boom!*
I hope I'm not alone
In this petrifying room.

I thought I smelt a monster
That smelled like rotten eggs.
It was very horrifying
You could see by my legs!

I thought I touched a monster
A very hairy one too.
Oh no, oh no...
I need to go to the loo.

I thought I could taste a monster
That was like a jar of pickles
Ha ha ha ha
I'm getting the giggles.

Nanw MacIntyre Huws (8)
Ysgol Brynaerau, Pontllyfni

Beware! Monsters Inside!

I thought I saw a monster,
A tiny but scary one
Looking through my window,
He scared everyone.

I thought I heard a monster
Going *swish, buzz, boom.*
I was petrified
So I hid in my room.

I thought I smelt a monster
Hiding under my bed,
Eating rotten eggs
While banging his head.

I thought I had touched a monster
He was hairy, slimy and fat,
He was as strong as a gorilla
But he looked like a cat.

I thought I could taste a monster,
I was terrified,

I couldn't believe my eyes,
I will be forever terrified.

Lleucu Haf Williams (10)
Ysgol Brynaerau, Pontllyfni

Sloppy The Monster

I thought I saw a monster
Underneath my bed,
It was hairy and scary
Just like my head.

It was small but fat
And it gave me a fright.
Suddenly I heard a bang
And I thought there was going to be a fight.

It ran through the door
And I ran as fast as lightning.
I could not believe my eyes,
It was petrifying.

Suddenly I went downstairs
And I saw it eating
Chocolate in the cupboard
That was for Mum's meeting.

At last Mum and Dad came home
To save me from the monster

It ran out to the street
Then we never saw the creature.

Sara Carroll (8)
Ysgol Brynaerau, Pontllyfni

Jeff From Space!

I thought I saw a monster
In the pitch-black woods
He wasn't very hairy
And wasn't very good.

I thought I saw a monster
Underneath my bed
I'm sure he was eating
Old and rotten bread.

Then I heard a bang!
While he was exploring my room.
I cuddled my pillow like a baby
Then there was a high-pitched boom!

He was getting closer and closer,
I hid under my bed.
Then he ran away by tripping over my bed,
I heard a big roar!

Then he came back
And smacked the door.

He was Jeff the alien!
Then I said, "Go, go, go!"

Rhydian Hildige (9)
Ysgol Brynaerau, Pontllyfni

The Weird Monster

I thought I saw a hairy monster
Under my comfy bed,
Smelly, creepy and green like lime
With one eye on his forehead.

He was sweaty, also gross
With sharp teeth like knives.
His fingernails were yellow,
I was scared for my life!

I heard the door creak
And heard bouncing. *Boom!*
I thought he had left,
But he was still in the room!

I ran down the noisy stairs
Like a wolf on the mountains,
It was like a fair in the kitchen
With flying cups, saucers and tins.

The monster went crazy
And I wanted to scream,

Luckily I woke up,
It was only a dream.

Betsan Cim Evans (10)
Ysgol Brynaerau, Pontllyfni

Stink The Stinky Monster

I thought I saw a monster
Underneath my bed,
He was a hairy and stinky one
That looked like he was dead.

I thought I heard a monster
Crawling through my door,
His tongue was as big as a razor,
I thought I was going into war.

I thought I smelt a monster
As stinky as the loo,
As I reached the bathroom
He shouted, "Boo!"

I thought I had touched a monster
Underneath my chair,
He felt like a lobster
Slobbering on my hair.

I thought I had tasted a monster,
My breath smelt like a dump,

I couldn't believe what happened,
I really wanted to jump.

Lily Erin Millen (8)
Ysgol Brynaerau, Pontllyfni

Fredo The Monster

I thought I heard a monster
Underneath my bed,
His teeth were like a blade
I thought I was dead.

I thought I smelt a monster
Growling in the closet,
I thought I saw him, using metal weapons,
He ate a lot of chocolate.

I saw something wiggling his tail,
Swish, splash, boom!
I locked all the doors
And windows in my room.

If Mum and Dad found out,
They would scream down the house,
Especially when they saw
That he looked like an enormous vicious mouse.

I thought I saw a monster
And he gave me a fright,

I thought he saw me,
I was ready for a fight.

Morgan Llyr Davies (9)
Ysgol Brynaerau, Pontllyfni

Catrin The Friendly Monster

I thought I saw a monster
Dancing under my bed,
I think she was eating bananas
While cuddling my teddy, Ted.

I thought I heard a monster
Whistling around the room,
She sounded like birds in the morning,
Then she ran quickly to the bathroom.

I thought I smelt a monster
But really it wasn't smelly,
She had beautiful lovely wings,
Then she started to watch the telly.

I thought I had touched a monster,
She was smooth like a baby,
Then I heard a *swish, swish, boom,*
In her hair was a tiny daisy.

I thought I could taste a monster
That tasted like an ice cream,
Then Mother came home
And gave a loud scream.

Elan Llyfni Fon Jones (8)
Ysgol Brynaerau, Pontllyfni

Vicky The Vicious Monster

I thought I saw a monster
Creeping up the stairs,
He looked like a strong one,
I thought he was eating pears.

He was coming even closer,
I could hear a *swish, swish, boom!*
I thought it was his tail,
I hid at the back of the room.

His nails were as sharp as a razor,
He was very, very stinky,
His teeth were disgustingly yellow,
He looked like his footprints were inky.

I could hear him quite clear,
He screamed, "Roar!"
He really, really frightened me,
Then I ran to the door.

His ears were as small as a mouse,
I could hear his footprints on the floor,

I was super petrified,
He was coming closer to the door.

Carys-Wyn Pass (9)
Ysgol Brynaerau, Pontllyfni

Watch Out, There's A Monster About

There's a monster in my head,
There's a monster in my bed,
There's a monster in the hall,
There's even a monster in the wall.

I thought I saw a monster giving me daunting looks,
I thought I saw a monster in-between my books,
I thought, *is there a monster in the house?*
If there was, Mum and Dad would bounce!

Every evening I lay in my bed at night,
I heard *swish, boom, bang.*
The thought of it gave me a fright
Till I ran to turn on my light.

I saw a monster in my mind
And then I thought I was blind,
Then I tried to find my mind.

Then I went back to bed
With everything in my head.

I thought I touched a monster,
He was the imposter.

Kimberly Jones (9)
Ysgol Brynaerau, Pontllyfni

The Nutella-Looking Slime Blob

I thought I saw a monster underneath my bed,
It was lying down on the floor as it was dead.
I thought I heard a roar coming from downstairs,
Was it a monster or was it bears?

I thought I saw a monster playing in the closet,
There was slime everywhere, I heard a bang like a rocket.
I thought I heard a swish and then a massive thump,
I hope there is a monster otherwise I will jump.

I thought I heard a monster having a bath in the bathroom,
Then he stamped his gruesome feet, *boom! Boom! Boom!*
I saw his teeth and they were razor-sharp,
Then I heard a bang, was it a monster or was it a falling harp?

I thought I smelt a monster coming from
downstairs,
Then I saw it and it was as hairy as a bear!
It came in my room, I was crying on the mat,
Then I realised it was Tommy the fat cat.

Arawn Dylan Morus (10)

Ysgol Brynaerau, Pontllyfni

Horrifying Monsters

A vicious monster broke into my house,
It sounded like a big deadly mouse,
I heard it coming up the stairs,
I blocked my door with lots of chairs.

As it crept across the hallway
I started screaming loudly, "Go away!"
I heard its tail going *swish, swish, boom!*
I hid under the bed in my room.

I heard a crazy noise going *bang, bang, bang!*
Was there more than one? Was there a gang?
I felt petrified and I hid under my bed,
I squished my teddy called Ted.

They tried pushing the door to get in,
So then I pushed back with my bin.
They were very strong compared to me,
Will they ever give up and let me be?

The door went swish and they came in,
I closed my eyes and hid behind the bin.

Suddenly, they touched me, I was going mad,
Then I noticed they were Mum and Dad.

Meilir Rhun Davies (9)
Ysgol Brynaerau, Pontllyfni

YoungWriters Est. 1991

YOUNG WRITERS INFORMATION

We hope you have enjoyed reading this book – and that you will continue to in the coming years.

If you're a young writer who enjoys reading and creative writing, or the parent of an enthusiastic poet or story writer, do visit our website **www.youngwriters.co.uk**. Here you will find free competitions, workshops and games, as well as recommended reads, a poetry glossary and our blog. There's lots to keep budding writers motivated to write!

If you would like to order further copies of this book, or any of our other titles, then please give us a call or order via your online account.

Young Writers
Remus House
Coltsfoot Drive
Peterborough
PE2 9BF
(01733) 890066
info@youngwriters.co.uk

Join in the conversation!
Tips, news, giveaways and much more!

YoungWritersUK   @YoungWritersCW